wind

Honor Head

QED Publishing

First published in the UK in 2006 by
QED Publishing
A Quarto Group company
226 City Road
London EC1V 2TT
www.qed-publishing.co.uk

A Catalogue record for this book is available from the British Library.

ISBN 978 1 84538 634 4

Written by Honor Head
Designed by Melissa Alaverdy
Consultant Terry Jennings
Editor Hannah Ray
Picture Researcher Joanne Forrest Smith
Illustrations Chris Davidson

Publisher Steve Evans
Editorial Director Jean Coppendale
Art Director Zeta Davies

Printed and bound in China

Picture credits

Key: t = top, b = bottom, c = centre,
l = left, r = right, FC = front cover

Alamy/Roger Bamber 11, /John Henshall 10;
Corbis/Owen Franken 5, /Mark Gamba FC,
/John Henley 8b, /Mark A Johnson 8–9,
/James Marshall 6, /Roy Morsch 18–19,
/Neil Rabinowitz 7, /Galen Rowell 12,
/Richard Hamilton Smith 4, /Wild Country 19t,
/Jim Zuckerman 13;
Ecoscene/Sally Morgan 15;
Getty Images/Martin Barraud 14,
/GK & Vikki Hart 2–3, /David Tipling 17t;
NHPA/Stephen Dalton 16–17.

Words in **bold** can be found in the glossary on page 22.

Contents

What is Wind?

Wind is air that is moving.

You cannot see wind, but you can feel the wind on your face. You can see the wind moving clouds in the sky. You can hear the wind blowing the leaves on a tree.

The wind is blowing the barley in this field.

If the wind is strong, it can blow your hair about!

In hot summer weather, wind helps to keep you cool. In the winter, the wind can be very cold and you have to wrap up warmly when you go outside.

How Do We Use Wind?

We use wind for all sorts of different things.

When we hang the washing outside, the wind helps to dry it. Wind also keeps flags flying. Without the wind, they would just hang down.

We use **wind turbines** to make electricity to light and heat people's homes. When the wind turns the sails of the turbines, they make electricity. The more the wind blows, the more electricity the turbines make.

Lots of wind turbines together are called a wind farm.

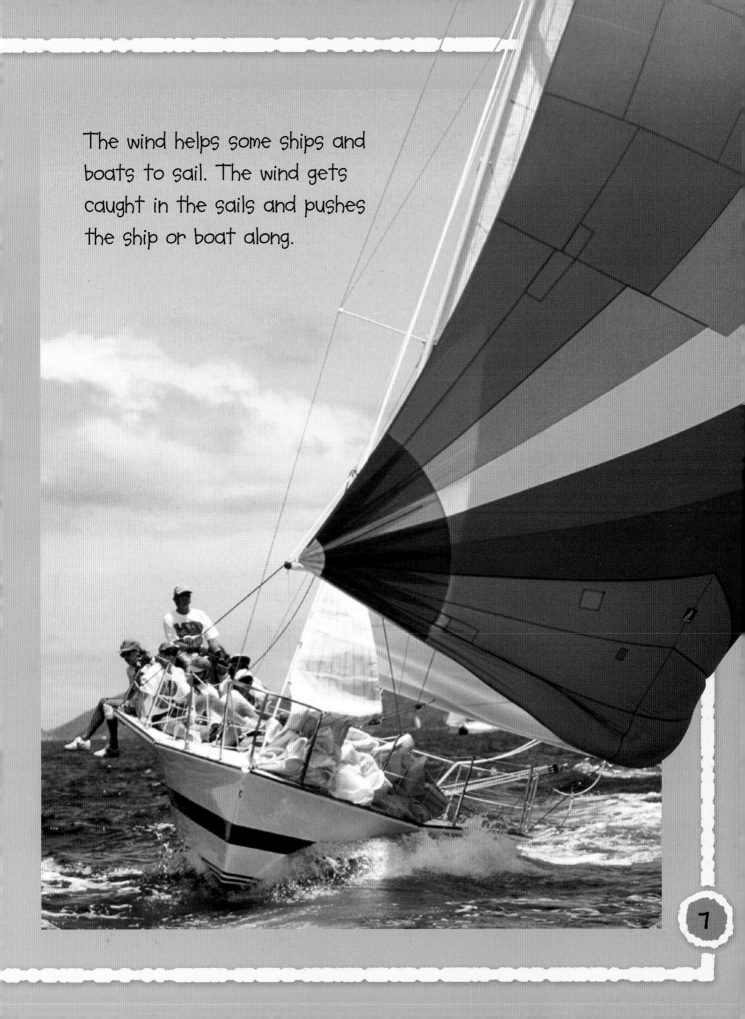

The wind helps some ships and boats to sail. The wind gets caught in the sails and pushes the ship or boat along.

Feel the Breeze

A light wind is sometimes called a **breeze**.

A breeze may make the leaves on the trees flutter and the grass move. We usually feel a breeze on warm spring or summer days.

If you are playing outside on a warm day, a breeze helps to keep you cool.

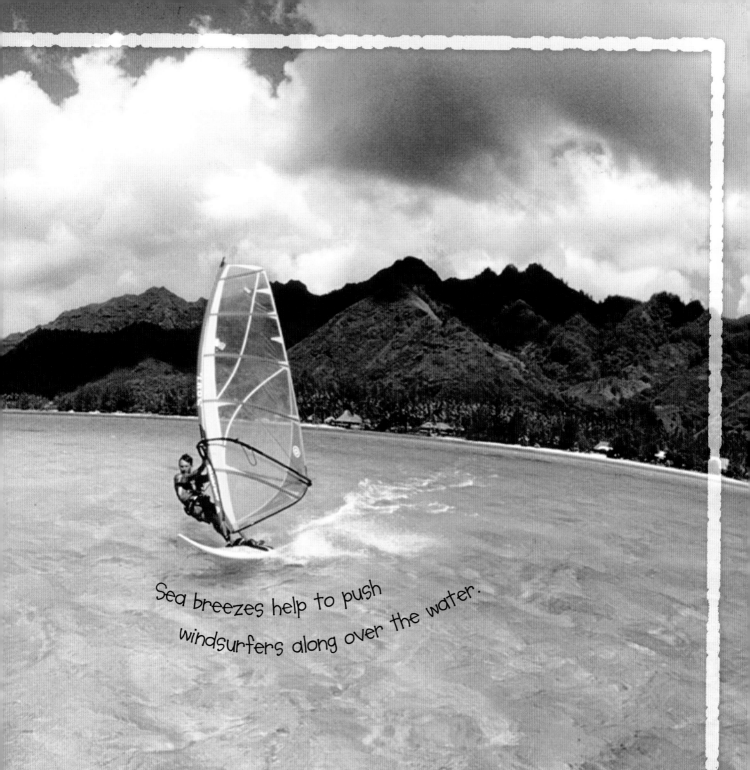

Sea breezes help to push windsurfers along over the water.

When air warms up it gets lighter and rises into the sky. Cooler air moves in to take its place. This cooler air is the breeze that we feel.

Gale Force

You know there is a strong wind when the branches on the trees toss from side to side.

It can be difficult to talk if a strong wind is blowing in your face. A very strong wind is called a gale.

Gales can break branches and can even blow down old trees.

A gale can make large
waves on the sea.

Hurricanes and Tornadoes

Some winds are so strong that they can cause a lot of damage.

The most powerful winds are called hurricanes. A hurricane happens when **storm clouds** build up over warm seas and get bigger and bigger. A hurricane can bring heavy rain and huge waves.

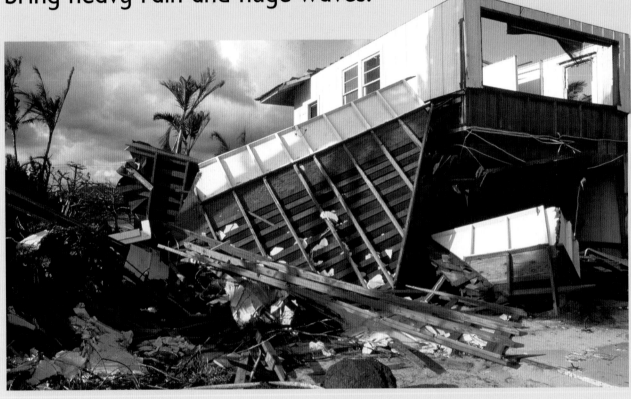

A hurricane is strong enough to blow down houses and turn cars upside-down.

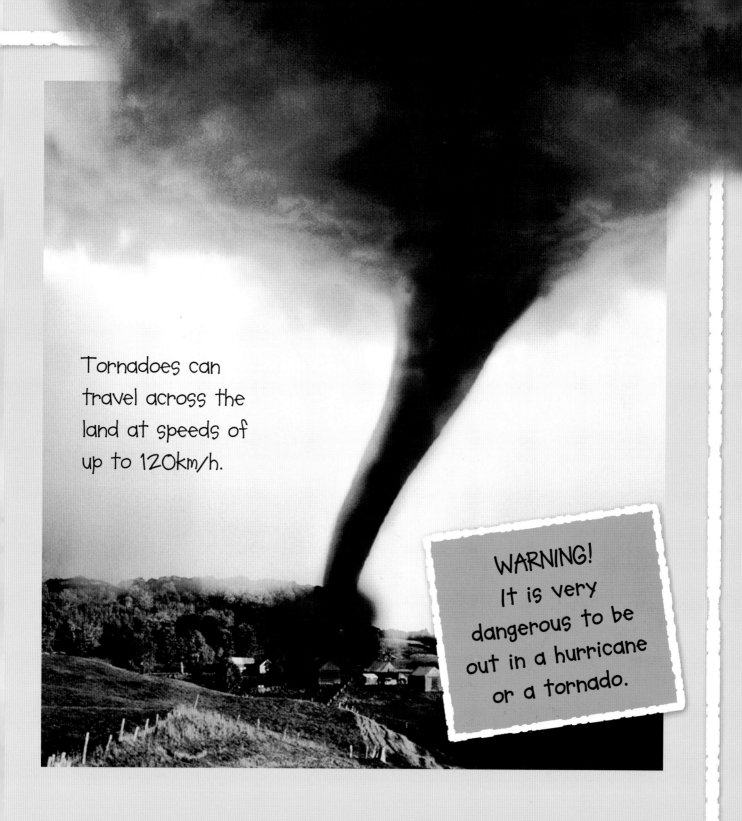

Tornadoes can travel across the land at speeds of up to 120km/h.

WARNING!
It is very dangerous to be out in a hurricane or a tornado.

A tornado is a funnel of wind that hangs down from a dark thunder cloud. This swirling cloud is like a vacuum cleaner – it sucks up everything in its path.

Wind and Plants

Many plants need the wind to help them to spread their pollen or seeds.

To make new plants, **pollen** from one flower has to move to another flower of the same kind. This is usually done by bees and other insects, but some plants use the wind to spread their pollen.

Dandelion seeds are spread when the wind blows on the plant. The seeds float in the air and land in the soil, where they grow into new plants.

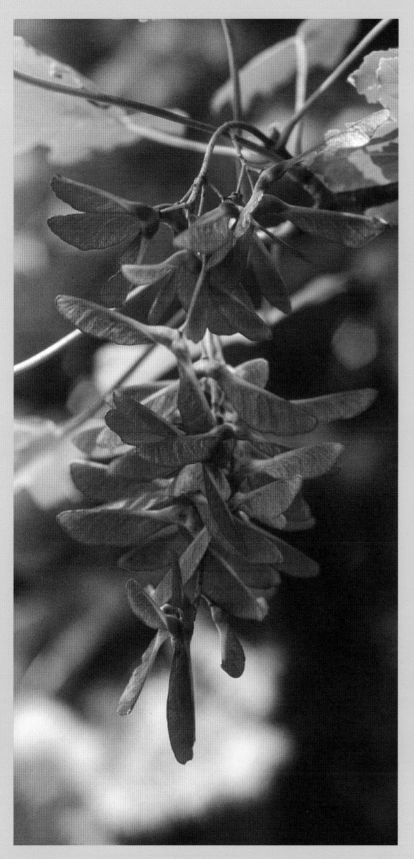

Some trees and plants have special seeds that use the wind to travel and spread. These seeds are very light and are easily picked up by the wind and carried away.

Trees such as this sycamore have seeds with wings. The wings help the seeds to stay in the air longer and travel further.

On the Wing

Animals also make use of the wind. Many large birds use the wind to help them fly.

Birds with big wings, such as this bald eagle, use the wind to help lift them into the air.

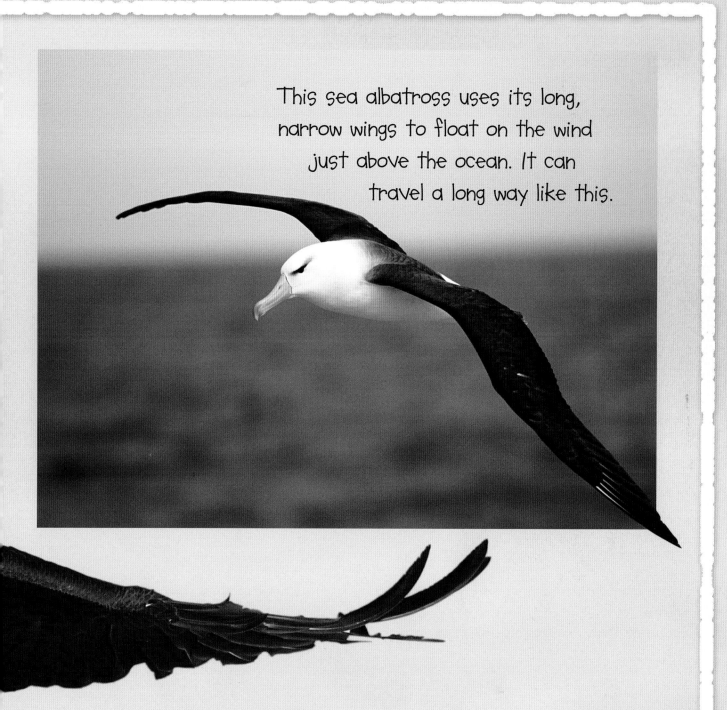

This sea albatross uses its long, narrow wings to float on the wind just above the ocean. It can travel a long way like this.

Birds can use their large wings to help them to **glide** on the wind for many kilometres. This means they don't have to flap their wings so much and they don't get so tired.

Windy Weather Fun

There are lots of fun things you can do using the wind.

Many people go to the top of a hill to fly kites, as the wind is usually stronger higher up.

The wind helps to lift your kite into the air.

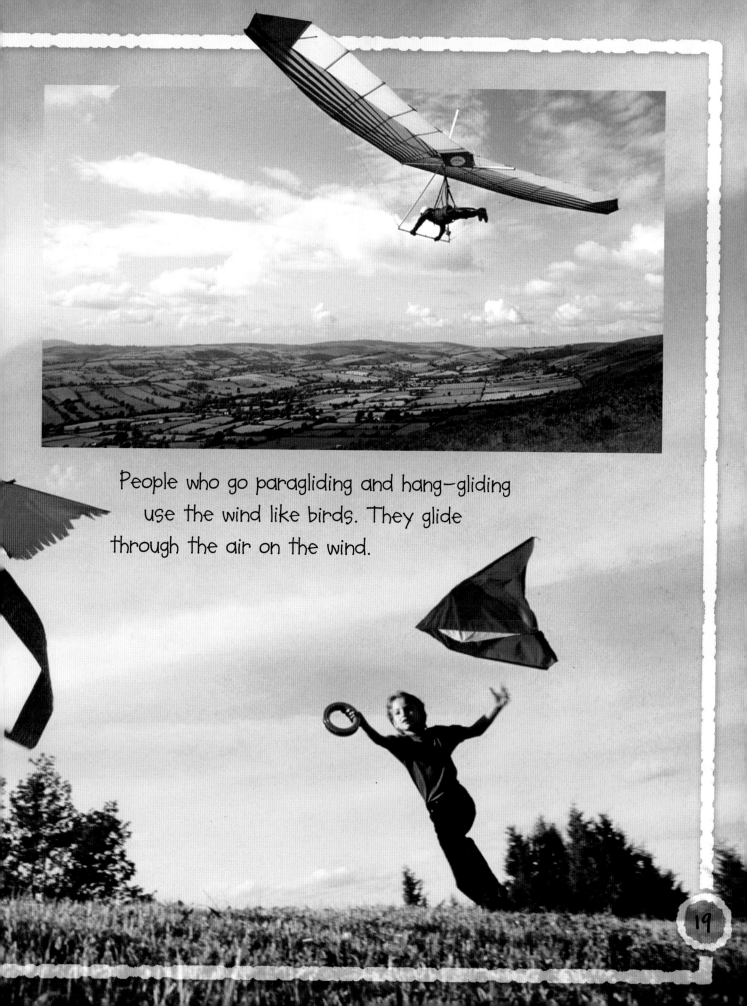

People who go paragliding and hang-gliding
use the wind like birds. They glide
through the air on the wind.

Make a Pinwheel

Make a pinwheel and see the wind move for yourself.

1. Decide how big you want your pinwheel to be and find a square of thick paper that size. You will also need a thin piece of wood, or bamboo, for the handle of your pinwheel.

2. Paint or draw a bright pattern onto both sides of your square of paper. Fold your square, corner to corner, then unfold. Fold the other two corners together, and unfold again.

3. Make a pencil mark along the fold lines, about halfway from the centre of the square.

4. Cut along the fold lines, stopping at your pencil marks. Fold each point into the centre of the pinwheel. Ask an adult to fix a drawing pin through all four points to hold the corners together.

5. Turn the wheel to make sure it will spin around the pin.

6. Push the drawing pin into the top of the handle.

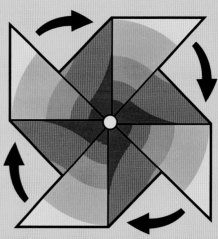

7. Stand in the wind and watch your pinwheel spin.

Glossary

breeze   a light wind that you usually feel
                 on a hot summer's day.

glide   when a bird moves through the air
                 without flapping its wings. It uses the
                 wind to push it along.

pollen   the yellow dust inside flowers that
                 helps the plant to grow new seeds.

storm clouds tall, dark clouds that usually bring
                 heavy rain and strong winds.

wind turbines tall, white towers with sails that are
                 turned by the wind to make electricity.
                 They look a bit like windmills.

Index

Parents' and Teachers' Notes

- Look at the cover of the book. Discuss the title and the picture on the cover. What do the children expect to see in the book? Are they looking forward to reading the book?

- Look through the book. Point out the captions to the photographs. Explain that captions give us more information about the photos.

- Find the contents, glossary and index pages. Explain the purpose of these to the children.

- Talk about the different types of wind. What is the wind like today? Look out of the window. Are the clouds moving quickly? Can you see trees moving? What else can you see that is being moved by the wind?

- Which season do the children associate with wind? For example, summer breezes or autumn winds blowing the leaves off trees.

- Do the children like the wind? Is it fun? Scary? Uncomfortable?

- Talk about how the children know it is windy. When can they hear it/see it/feel it?

- Choose a selection of different weight materials, such as woollen scarves, cotton handkerchiefs or headscarves, tea towels and bath towels. On a windy day, take the children outside and ask them to hold up the materials. Which ones fly in the wind? Do the same experiment when the wind is stronger or weaker. If the wind is stronger, do the heavier materials start to fly?

- Point out that the wind does not always come from the same direction. Look for weather vanes and windsocks. Make a model weather vane or windsock.

- Draw a sky full of kites. Ask each child to draw and decorate a kite and put them all up on a wall against a blue-sky background. Add strings to each kite.